The Bakewell Ottoman Garden

The Bakewell Ottoman Garden

AT THE MISSOURI BOTANICAL GARDEN

by Prof. Nurhan Atasoy and Philippa Scott

foreword by Dr. Peter H. Raven

MISSOURI BOTANICAL GARDEN

SAINT LOUIS, MISSOURI

Photography as credited throughout. Historical photo (page 33) from the Missouri Botanical Garden Archives. Visit www.mobot.org to view an illustrated history of the Garden online. Historical Ottoman images from *A Garden for the Sultan* (pages 5, 8, 14, 16–34, 42, 60) used with permission by Nurhan Atasoy.

ABOUT THE AUTHORS

Nurhan Atasoy

Resident scholar of the Turkish Cultural Foundation in Istanbul, Atasoy is an art historian specializing in Ottoman art. After receiving her Ph.D. from Istanbul University, she served as faculty, Department Chair, and eventually Dean of the Faculty of Letters there before retiring in 1999. Atasoy has presented at conferences and symposia around the world and received numerous awards and honorary titles. She has publication credits for 80 articles and 20 books, including *Iznik: Ottoman Pottery of Turkey* (with Julian Raby), *The Art of Islam* (with A. Bahnassi and M. Rogers), *Otağı Hümayun: Imperial Ottoman Tents, IPEK: Imperial Ottoman Silks and Velvets*, and *A Garden for the Sultan: Gardens and Flowers in the Ottoman Culture*. Her text in this volume is edited by Yasemin Irepoğlu.

Philippa Scott

London-based author and freelance journalist, Philippa Scott is a contributing editor to *Hali* magazine, the leading English-language periodical devoted to oriental rugs, textiles, and Islamic art. Scott's book credits include: *The Book of Silk, Turkish Delights*, and *Gourmet Game*. She also contributed to *Reflections of Paradise, The Englishwoman's Kitchen, India of the Rajahs, Meetings with Remarkable Muslims, Syria Through Writers' Eyes*, and the *Insight Guide to the Silk Road*.

ISBN: 978-0-615-39205-9
Editor: Elizabeth McNulty
Designer: Alexandria Martinez
♻ Printed on 100% post-consumer recycled paper.

Cover photo: *In the Bakewell Ottoman Garden, a traditional Ottoman sundial (center) at the entrance reminds visitors of the passage of time—and of the times for prayer in Muslim culture. The central fountain is of paramount importance: water was acknowledged as the source of life in Ottoman culture. (Photo by Leslie Wallace.)*

Page 1: *Mural paintings of roses, carnations, tulips, and other flowers on the walls of the Bakewell Ottoman Garden evoke the famous botanical illustrations of renowned Ottoman floral painter Ali Üsküdari. (Photo by Jeffrey Ricker.)*

Previous page: *A view of the Sultan's throne in the Bakewell Ottoman Garden overlooking the central havuz, or shallow pool of water, around which jets of water play. In the foreground are traditional beds of boldly colored Dianthus. (Photo by Laila Wessel.)*

Page 64: *Edward L. Bakewell, Jr., the Benefactor. (Photo by Kristen Peterson.)*

table of contents

foreword BY DR. PETER H. RAVEN

Dr. Peter H. Raven.
(Photo by Kristi Foster.)

The story of the Ottoman Empire touches the United States in serendipitous ways. For example, an Ottoman sultan contributed toward the building of the Washington Monument. Visitors to that famous obelisk today may still see, set high inside the stairs, a marble plaque of the imperial signature in gold leaf. The story of the Ottoman Empire touches the Missouri Botanical Garden too. The Garden's founder, St. Louis businessman Henry Shaw, toured Europe and the Mediterranean in 1841, spending nearly two months in what is now Turkey. In his journals, reprinted on the Garden's "Travels with Henry" blog, Shaw documents the dress and manner of Turkish men and women, the honesty of the Turkish porters, the mosques, and "Dancing Dervishes." He even buys a Turkish carpet! Being interested in plants and gardens, he also writes about the local flora (honeysuckle, oleander, and cypress) and the kiosks and summer houses that dot the sultan's gardens at the Topkapi Palace.

How wonderful that the story of the Ottoman Empire also touches the family of Edward L. Bakewell, Jr., and how appropriate that his sons, Ted and Duke, elected to share that story with the community by building the Bakewell Ottoman Garden.

Turkey is the place where East meets West, and the Ottoman Empire introduced hundreds of plants to Western Europe. To name but a few: chionodoxa (glories-of-the-snow), crocuses, hyacinths, opium poppy, weeping willow, tulips, hollyhocks, and horticulturally important species of snowdrop, daffodil, iris, lily, daylily, peony, ranunculus, and rhododendrons. The list goes on and on, and many may be seen in the Bakewell Ottoman Garden.

Gardens epitomize nature and were symbols of paradise to the Ottomans. The Bakewell Ottoman Garden at the Missouri Botanical Garden provides a beautiful setting for peaceful contemplation of the history of East-West dialog—and perhaps a place to start new dialogs today. In this way, the garden fulfills the vision of founder Henry Shaw, who created his garden "for all time for the public good."

Outside these old stone walls, Missouri Botanical Garden botanists and our partners are working to document and preserve plants around the world. All life on Earth depends on plants, and many are very poorly known. Yet, by the end of the century, half of the estimated 400,000 species of plants could be extinct in nature or on the way to extinction. As many as 100,000 more species of plants await discovery. Which among them could provide the next life-saving medicine? Please consider supporting the Missouri Botanical Garden in this great effort.

Peter H. Raven

Dr. Peter H. Raven
President of the Missouri Botanical Garden

Today in every country on Earth, species are becoming extinct at an unprecedented rate. The work of Missouri Botanical Garden scientists creates the foundation for conservation, and community-based efforts empower local populations to protect the future of biodiversity for us all. Your membership in the Missouri Botanical Garden benefits these important conservation programs. Learn more at www.mobot.org.

chapter I   INTRODUCTION TO THE BAKEWELL OTTOMAN GARDEN

BY PHILIPPA SCOTT

The Bakewell Ottoman Garden is located in the northeast corner of the Missouri Botanical Garden in St. Louis, Missouri. Opened in 2006 and formally dedicated on May 16, 2008, it is not just the first garden of its kind in the United States, but is the only known public Ottoman garden in the world. Together with the Japanese and Chinese gardens already established, the Ottoman Garden allows the Missouri Botanical Garden to present Near Eastern, Far Eastern, and Western garden traditions simultaneously as never before in a beautiful and significant presentation to the general public. The designers hope that this fascinating garden will help to develop an understanding of Ottoman history. Visitors previously unaware of the extensive Ottoman contribution to the history of gardening and botanical studies will be surprised, and it is hoped that this previously neglected aspect of garden history will inspire and stimulate others, thus helping to resurrect a distinct and individual

An Ottoman sundial stands at the entrance to the Bakewell Ottoman Garden. On it, visitors can read Western European, Italian, and Babylonian time. (Photo by Laila Wessel.)

gardening tradition in its own right. The imperial city of Constantinople, now renamed Istanbul, lies on an equivalent latitude to St. Louis, and although their continental situations and climate differ in some respects, many of the same plants will flourish in the gardens of each city.

The Origins of the Bakewell Ottoman Garden

The Bakewell Ottoman Garden is a walled garden, an enclosed space, a retreat, made possible by a generous gift from the late Edward L. Bakewell, Jr. It began with a romantic family legend linking the Bakewells to the Ottoman dynasty of the late 18th and early 19th century. When charged with executing their father's wish to create a legacy garden within the Missouri Botanical Garden, his sons recalled how a visit to Istanbul in the 1970s had rekindled their father and mother's curiosity.

Through the maternal line, the Bakewell family are said to be related to Aimée Dubucq de la Rivery, a young girl born in Martinique in the late 18th century. Sent to France to complete her education, in 1788 she was returning to the island when her ship was wrecked in a storm. According to various novels and a number of highly romanticized films, Aimée was rescued from an abrupt and watery end and passed through the hands of a famous pirate captain, taken to Algiers, and then to Istanbul where she was presented as a gift to the sultan and found herself installed in the imperial harem. She is believed to have been renamed Nakshidil, the woman who became the mother of the future Sultan Mahmud II. (Mahmud II went on to conclude the first trade treaty between the Ottoman Empire and the United States of America in 1830.)

Mystery still surrounds the story of Aimée Dubucq, but certainly the women in the sultan's harem, and consequently the mothers of the sultans, were always non-Turkish. This avoided any attempts at influence by ambitious relatives, and the women were completely dependent on their sultan. Once a woman had a son, her life was devoted to his upbringing. *Harem* means "sanctuary," and the imperial harem was the women's quarters; the sultans' concubines and female slaves lived there. The harem was a world within a world, and the palace gardens were laid out in a series of terraces, open spaces, and enclosed walled gardens (gardens within gardens), allowing privacy.

Aimée's cousin and island playmate, Marie-Josephe-Rose de Tascher de la Pagerie, was also sent to France, but her life followed a different path. Renamed Josephine by her second husband, the Emperor Napoleon, she created a famous garden at Malmaison. Among the many roses she planted was the dark violet beauty 'La Belle Sultane' (the Beautiful Sultana), also referred to as 'Rose du Serail' (Rose of the Imperial Harem). In creating her rose garden Josephine alluded to her own original name, Rose, and that of her mother, Rose-Claire; in planting 'La Belle Sultane' it is tempting to read a reference to her cousin Aimée, and her life in the splendor and luxury of the imperial seraglio and the secluded gardens of the Topkapi. In its way, the Bakewell Ottoman Garden is another chapter in Aimée Dubucq's romantic history.

Roses are an important part of Ottoman culture, and their sweet fragrance fills the Bakewell Ottoman Garden on warm summer days. The arbor in the background shades murals of roses and other flowers important to the Ottomans. (Photo by Kristen Peterson.)

The Ottoman Empire lasted for some 500 years, and the Bakewell Ottoman Garden takes its lead from Aimée's era, the 18th and 19th centuries. By this time, Europe's great fear of the vast empire on its borders had given way to fascination with all things Ottoman. Fashionable people posed in Ottoman dress to have their portraits painted, Turkish tents and pavilions were featured in parks and gardens, music was composed "alla Turca," interiors were decorated in "Turkish" style, and it was all the rage to relax in Turkish baths, drink coffee—the Turkish drink—and recline on divans and "ottomans" in exotic smoking rooms to smoke Turkish cigarettes. The principal sitting room inside an Ottoman waterside mansion, *yalı*, was called "sofa."

All gardens are reminders that time does not stand still; change is inevitable. The Ottoman Empire was also changing. Illustrations and designs of famous European royal gardens were studied in Istanbul, European gardeners were recruited, Ottoman landscaping practices were overtaken gradually by European fashion, and sultans listened to French and Italian operas while sipping Champagne.

Water gently drips along tiers of the selsebil, *or wall fountain, in the Bakewell Ottoman Garden. It was made by traditional craftsmen in Turkey from Turkish marble. (Photo by Todd Gilbert.)*

chapter II HISTORICAL OVERVIEW

BY PROF. NURHAN ATASOY

TURKS AND OTTOMANS

For a variety of reasons and changing circumstances, Turkish tribes in their ancestral heartland of Central Asia began to move westward from the 6th century onward. By the late 10th century, when the main migration took place, they began to favor the teachings and practices of Islam over their native shamanism. There were many tribal groups, of which the more forceful and successful established their own states. In Asia Minor, the Seljuk Turks won a significant victory over the Byzantine army at Manzikert (Malazgirt) in 1071. They settled in Anatolia, and their capital was Konya.

Toward the end of the 13th century, a small tribe of Turks with an ambitious young leader, Osman Gazi (*gazi* means warrior), emerged on the scene. Gaining territories and experience, making diplomatic marriages, they eventually became the most powerful force in the region. They were known as the Osmanli or Ottoman Turks. Their first capital was Bursa, the next Edirne, and it was from Edirne that the twenty-one-year-old Sultan Mehmed II marched the Ottoman army to lay siege to the great Byzantine capital, Constantinople, in 1452. In May 1453 the city, and the once great empire, fell to this new power. All remaining Byzantine territories became Ottoman, Constantinople was renamed Istanbul and became the capital of what was destined to become one of the greatest of all world empires, that of the Ottomans, joining Europe and Asia.

Mehmed II ruled from 1451 until his death in 1481. His grandson, Selim I, (r. 1512–1520) looked eastward. He took Syria in 1516, captured Tabriz, and conquered Egypt in 1517. The Ottoman capital was enriched by skilled artisans and works of art from all of these

territories. The Ottoman Empire became Protector of the Holy Cities of Mecca and Medina, and as such elevated to the center of the Islamic world.

Eventually, during the long reign of Suleyman I (1520–1566), the empire reached its largest territorial range. Under competent rulership, his campaigns forged mainly westward; he captured a large part of Hungary, laid siege to Vienna, and conquered most of the North African coast. To the West, Suleyman was known as "the Magnificent," but to his subjects he was Kanuni or "the lawgiver." Suleyman participated in Christian politics, allying with France and the Protestant German princes against Holy Roman Emperor Charles V.

This period witnessed the height of Ottoman power and expansion. Over the next three hundred years, territories were slowly lost. The empire's rapid expansion paved the way for its eventual dissolution; borders were remote and the administration of such an extensive territory became too difficult. The Ottoman's initial military superiority was superceded by technical advancements in Europe. A period of slow decline punctuated occasionally by attempts at reform gradually led to the slow dissolution of this great empire. The 19th century saw break-away states formed in the Balkans, Greece seized independence, and bit by bit other territories were ceded to foreign powers. After World War I, and some five hundred years as a world power, the Ottoman Empire was dissolved. Under the leadership of Mustafa Kemal, known as Ataturk, "the Father of the Nation," the modern Republic of Turkey was founded in 1923, and a new era began. Today, Turkey is a secular, democratic state.

OTTOMAN GARDEN CULTURE

Roses were especially prized by the Ottomans for their fragrance, as well as for the eau-de-vie made from their petals.

As Turks emigrated westward from Central Asia, they encountered different climatic conditions, peoples, cultures, traditions, and architecture. They introduced many indigenous Central Asian plants to areas of what are now Iran and Turkey, where they eventually settled. This great expanse of land stretching between Asia and Europe, situated at the junction of what botanists call the Eurosiberian and Irano-Turanian zones, is extraordinarily rich from a botanical perspective.

Horticulture and botany were quite advanced in the Islamic world, far more so than in the West at that time. Works by ancient authors had survived by being translated into Arabic, and new major works were written by Arab scholars. Three Ottoman sultans are particularly associated with flowers and gardens: Mehmed II, "the Conqueror" (r. 1451–1481), his great-grandson, Suleyman I, "the Magnificent" (r. 1520–1566), and Ahmed III (r. 1703–1730), whose reign is known as "the Tulip Era." Unfortunately, no information exists about Ottoman garden culture before the time of Mehmed II. Such information might have revealed the origins of the sultan's love of gardens and interest in horticulture. Significantly, in his formal portrait, Mehmed II chose to have himself depicted not in martial pose, but seated, peaceably holding a rose and inhaling its scent.

Portrait of Sultan Mehmed II, "the Conqueror," smelling a rose. Mehmed II is one of three Ottoman sultans particularly associated with flowers and gardens. He reigned from 1451–1481.

(An archer's ring on his thumb is the only intimation of his military might.) He was a poet and knowledgeable patron of the arts with a keen interest in Western arts and culture, and his library contained a broad range of literature on many subjects in a variety of languages.

After the conquest of Constantinople, Mehmed II ordered a garden to be created at the spot where he had made his first encampment during the siege. Fountains, pools, and pavilions were constructed. Thousands of fruit trees, weeping willows, boxwood, stone pines, and twelve thousand cypresses were planted in a checkerboard pattern. The Sultan planted seven cypress trees with his own hands.

The city of Constantinople was in ruins, and immediate plans for reconstruction were set in motion. In the meantime, the Sultan and his retinue lived in a tented encampment. During the construction of the Topkapi Palace, which was to become the headquarters of administration and the house of the Sultan, Mehmed ordered gardens to be built on the slopes of the Seraglio Point by the sea on three sides. Although Constantinople, renamed Istanbul, was to be the new Ottoman capital, the previous capital, Edirne, remained a hunting destination and occasional resting place for Ottoman sultans. Mehmed ordered thousands of trees, fruit trees, and flowers to be planted in the gardens of Edirne Palace.

The laquered cover to a book of hadiths, *tales of the prophet Mohammed, circa 1540s. It depicts a paradise garden with blossoming trees and flowers.*

Like his great grandfather, Mehmed II, Suleyman the Magnificent (r. 1520–1566) is remembered for his military successes, and like his great grandfather, Suleyman was also a poet. Literary gatherings, readings, and performances often took place in gardens, and these events fostered the young sultan's love of gardens. His reign, at the height of Ottoman power and prestige, witnessed a flourishing of all branches of the arts, and the great Sinan was the royal architect.

Suleyman commissioned more than thirty gardens in Istanbul and the surrounding regions, and new floral motifs and patterns blossomed in carpets and textiles, ceramics, jewelry, metalwork, and stone. Previously, representations of flowers were stylized and hard to identify, but now court painters sought realism, and in the first half of the 16th century a new floral style emerged.

Native to China, carnations were domesticated in the eastern Mediterranean and rapidly adapted throughout Eurasia.

It was customary each spring for the sultan to embark on military campaigns, and the landscape and location of exceptional trees and flowers were noted. One archival document lists saplings of plane, ash, linden, mahaleb cherry, oak, elm, bay, redbud, wild pear, and similar trees in quantities of four thousand each were to be sent from distant areas to furnish gardens in and around Istanbul. A document from the reign of Suleyman I, dated 1526, mentions purchase of "Kaffa tulips," as well as a large number of other unspecified flower species from Crimea, for the privy gardens. Another document, dated 1564, points out expenditures in great quantities, some of which were for "boxes of jasmines and carnations." Another, dated 1576, orders hyacinth bulbs from Aleppo, at that time Ottoman territory. In 1592, four hundred quintals (almost 25 tons!) of red roses, and another three hundred quintals of white roses from Edirne "as usual" were ordered, followed by an order for 100,000 hyacinth bulbs—50,000 white and 50,000 blue—for use in the palace gardens. The latter were to be obtained from "the mountains and meadows" in the city of Maras, in southeastern Anatolia.

An 18th century document setting out the replanting and redesigning of one of the palace gardens includes a list of requirements, which include 220 tubs of linden, carnations, "Frankish" roses, yellow roses, "Frankish" vines, jasmine, virgin's bower, and double Sweet Williams.

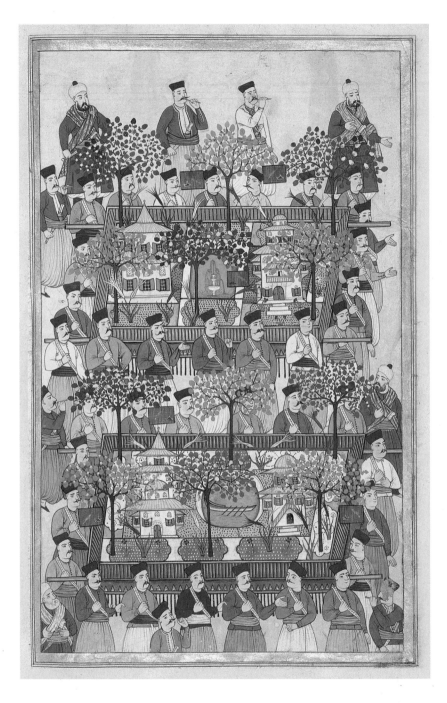

Detail of a painting by court artist Levni. Gardens were so central to Ottoman culture that during a festival in 1582, the Guild of Confectioners created miniature gardens from sugar and almond paste to please the Sultan and honor his son.

During the festivities surrounding the circumcision of the sons of Ahmed III in 1720, palace confectioners created models of gardens from sugar, and these were paraded for all to admire. In the miniature paintings depicting these celebrations may be seen four huge sugar gardens, modeled with garden kiosks, pools with fountains and little boats, trees heavy with fruit, the cypress trees without which no Ottoman garden was complete, and *parterres* of tulips and other flowers.

Between 1703 and 1716, the great botanist William Sherard was British Consul in Izmir, a city not far from Manisa (famous for its tulips). His house and garden were in the south of the city, at Seydiköy, on the road to Ephesus. The garden is thought to have played a key role in enabling many species of plant to reach England and English botanists through Sherard's brother.

As plants from the Ottoman Empire entered European gardens, gardens in Turkey began to change. During the reign of Ahmed III, bulbs and plants had begun to be exported from the Ottoman Empire to Europe, most notably tulips, the arrival of which caused much excitement in Holland. At the same time, Turkey began to study European garden design and ideas, incorporating some concepts into Ottoman gardens. This exchange began in the 18th and continued throughout the 19th centuries.

General Elements of Ottoman Gardens

Gardens undergo a process of continuous change and development; therefore, any study of their history must emphasize architectural elements and rely on contemporary visual and written materials showing their organization and layout.

Archival documents, together with the images found in miniature paintings, provide a clear picture of real Ottoman gardens and flowers. The structural elements of an

The Iznik-tiled walls of the Queen Mother's bedroom in the harem quarters of the Topkapi Palace depict stylized trees, vines, and flowers.

Ottoman garden were pavilions or kiosks, pools and fountains, and the much-loved cypress trees, all of which feature in miniature paintings and provide visual documentation.

A wonderful album preserved in the Topkapi Palace Library depicts an imperial festival in 1582, which lasted 52 days and 52 nights to celebrate the circumcision of Prince Mehmed, the son of Murad III (r. 1574–1595). Members of the various guilds displayed representations of their trades and skills: the florists carried huge circular wooden trays with vases filled with various flowers; the fruit-sellers carried trays filled with fruits; the gardeners displayed gardening tools and model gardens complete with cypresses and fountains.

The cover of the album Tercumani-I Destur *(1728) illuminated by court artist Abdullah Buhari. Set along the water's edge is a walled garden with a central kiosk and rectangular beds.*

Ottoman garden kiosks exhibited an enormous amount of diversity in their architectural features, and they ranged in size from modest bowers to luxurious pavilions. Rugs and cushions would be laid within as required. An important element of a garden pavilion was the way it was located, so as to offer the best possible view of its surroundings. By far the most important feature of an Ottoman garden pavilion was that it should be open to its surroundings and blend into the garden as if it were a part of nature. Throne-like Ottoman garden seats were usually designed to be portable so they could be set up wherever they were needed and furnished with cushions, pillows, coverings, and draperies made from precious fabrics.

A scene from an album of the reign of Ahmed I, early 17th century. A feasting figure sits on a small carpet in a garden and is served food by pages. In the background are cypresses and a tree in spring blossom with irises at the base. Flowers, possibly poppies, grow in the grass.

Ottoman gardens were not made according to fixed rules or rigid plans, but by practical solutions that suited the topography, garden dimensions, and climate. Instead of building watercourses, they created gardens where running water already existed, or by the seashore. They would create gardens benefitting from what nature had already provided by planting flowerbeds around existing trees. They made the best possible use of available land when determining the location of a garden and the construction of garden architecture. The placement of terraces and embankments and the layout of watercourses were never haphazard. As well as serving an aesthetic purpose, Ottoman gardens were both functional and practical, and herbs and vegetables were planted alongside flowers and fruit trees.

At Topkapi Palace, a large garden courtyard was devoted to ceremonies. All court officials were required to dress in their most dazzling garb and array themselves in protocol order, flanking the sultan's throne in what was tantamount to a theatrical set-piece. But many court gardens and private gardens, small or big in size, were also designed as places where the sultans and courtiers could enjoy some private time as well.

The Second Courtyard of the Topkapi Palace, illustration by the court artist Matrakci Nasuh, mid-1500s. The old palace is shown surrounded by a four-square high wall and a garden planted with many tall trees.

TRAVELERS AND OTTOMAN GARDENS

Most foreign visitors remarked upon the Ottoman love of flowers and gardens. "A few shady trees, a view, a rosebud, and the sound of a nightingale will transform any garden into a Turkish garden," said Father Stephan Gerlach, a Lutheran chaplain accompanying a Hapsburg delegation to the Sublime Porte in about 1576. He continued: "On the first and second terraces of the Seraglio there are many woods, vineyards, and orchards of every kind of fruit tree. Also in this area are kitchen gardens in which there exists every kind of fruit tree and every sort of flower and herb."

French Orientalist Pétis de La Croix (1653–1713), who spent time in Syria, Persia, Algiers, Morocco, Tunis, and Turkey, notes there were sixty-one gardens in 1600 within the palace, in which five hundred gardeners were employed. He also reports that this number increased to two thousand by 1677, and that "The holiday celebrating the arrival of spring would begin when the tulips blossomed and at this time, the gardens would be decorated with lanterns and other finery."

A painting of a woman holding a rose in her right hand and two carnations in her left hand by Levni, the greatest court artist of the Tulip Era, early 1700s.

Baron de Tott, an adviser on military matters who accompanied the French ambassador de Vergennes to Istanbul in 1755, said that tulips were very popular accompaniments to the evening parties held in the palace gardens and that a pleasurable atmosphere was created by their presence.

"There exists," he wrote, "every sort and fragrance of flower beneath the trees in the sultan's palace. The cypress is the most common type of tree. The Sultan strolls alone in his garden. The French party was taken to a paradise called The Garden of Luster, where there were long footpaths, cypress trees, flowers, fountains, and caverns. In addition, they also admitted us into the section for the newly recruited pages.

"...The aforementioned chambers and the buildings wherein the sultan resides have exquisite gardens in which there are flowers and fruit trees of every kind, lovely walkways shaded by tall cypresses on both sides, and a great many marble fountains. There are at least a few of these fountains along nearly every path.... The Sultan and all the Turks greatly enjoy such things. Indeed a Turk takes great pleasure in being in a fine garden during the summer and he satisfies his feelings in that way. As soon as he comes to such a place he will—if the place belongs to him or if he feels self-assured enough—remove his upper garments and set

them to one side.... During the sweet moments that he spends there, that garden is nothing less than a paradise. He will fill his arms with flowers and adorn his turban with flowers and then inhale their sweet fragrances. Occasionally he may come across a lovely flower bearing the same name as his beloved and then he will sing a song to it, crooning the words with the utmost ardor as if she were there herself. A bit of meat cooked in a garden seems better to him than the finest fare."

Ottoman Gardens & Plants in the Western World

The first wave of exotic plants to enter Europe in relatively modern times corresponds to the years following the publication of Pierre Belon's account of his travels in the Ottoman Empire in 1546–48. The French traveler observed the tulips, present in every Turkish garden, and described them as a kind of lily, noting that they were very different from those in his country.

A few years later, Ogier Ghiselin de Busbecq, Hapsburg ambassador to the Ottoman court from 1554 to 1562, was astonished by the variety of flowers in Ottoman gardens and brought back to Vienna an illustrated copy of Dioscorides' *De Materia Medica*, a book of ancient knowledge about medical plants, as well as bulbs and corms of tulips, hyacinths, anemones, and crown imperials. These he presented to his friend Charles de l'Escluse (Clusius). Clusius moved to Leiden, where he continued to share these specimens with his large circle of colleagues in various parts of Europe. From the 1560s onward crocuses, colchicums, leucojums, erythroniums, ornithogalums, cyclamens, alliums, hyacinths, lilies, fritillaries, ranunculi, and especially tulips began to find favor in many European gardens, and merchants were eager to supply this increasing demand. In 1562, a merchant from Amsterdam shipped the first recorded cargo of tulip bulbs from Istanbul to Europe.

Previous page: *In the harem quarters of Topkapi Palace, the cypress room is noted for the dramatic cypress motifs seen at right in the photograph. Flower-filled vases and pots and flower-covered vines complete the Iznik-tile design.*

Two bouquets from a series of flower portraits by famed 18th-century Ottoman floral artist Ali Üsküdari. At left, a Narcissus *and an "Algerian violet" (vinca). At right, a tulip with elongated petals of the type favored by the Turks and a pansy.*

A doctor who accompanied de Busbecq's embassy, Willem Quackelbeen, sent a note on "simples" to a Pietro Andrea Mattioli, detailed in notebooks kept by Ulisse Aldrovandi of the Bologna Botanical Garden from 1569 to 1602. Aldrovandi recorded letters, lists of seeds and plants, and other objects of natural interest he received from his vast circle of correspondents. Another entry lists a quantity of bulbs obtained for the Duke of Sermoneta in 1625, including "white narcissi from Constantinople."

Many ornamental plants are believed to have been popularized in Europe around this time as a result of Ottoman influence. For example, beautiful flowers were highly prized in Ottoman gardens, such as bulbous crown imperials (*Fritillaria imperialis*), hyacinths (*Hyacinthus orientalis*), tulips (*Tulipa* spp.), love-in-a-mist (*Nigella damascena*), and cultivated species of herbaceous anemone (*Anemone* spp.), daffodil (*Narcissus papyraceus*), ranunculus (*Ranunculus asiaticus*), iris (*Iris pallida, I. susiana*), and lily (*Lilium candidum, L. cernuum, L. chalcedonicum*). Woody ornamentals that also became popular included cherry laurel (*Prunus laurocerasus*), lilac (*Syringa persica*), mock orange (*Philadelphus coronarius*), and oleaster (*Eleagnus angustifolia*). When brought to European gardens, they joined valuable plants such as the Oriental plane tree (*Platanus orientalis*) and common walnut (*Juglans regia*), which had already been spread from southwest Asia to northwestern Europe by Roman times. Subsequent arrivals included black mulberry (*Morus nigra*) and indirectly the hollyhock (*Alcea* spp.), white jasmine (*Jasminum sambac*), scarlet lychnis (*Lychnis chalcedonica*), and opium poppy (*Papaver somniferum*).

The Ottoman influence could still be felt in European gardens continuing into the 17th, 18th, and 19th centuries, Ottoman favorites such as horse chestnut (*Aesculus hippocastanum*), cloth-of-gold crocus (*Crocus angustifolius*), Crimean snowdrop (*Galanthus plicatus*), Byzantine gladiolus (*Gladiolus communis* subsp. *byzantinus*), daylilies (*Hemerocallis* spp., mostly native to East Asia), and sweet sultan (*Amberboa moschata*) began to appear in the West. The cedar of Lebanon (*Cedrus libani*) made its way to Europe soon after 1650. Sir George Wheeler sent the first specimen of the Great St. John's wort (*Hypericum calycinum*) in 1676. Weeping willow (*Salix babylonica* or hybrids thereof, originally from China) arrived in 1692. In 1735, the Turkish oak (*Quercus cerris*) was first brought to England, followed by the common rhododendron (*Rhododendron ponticum*) in 1763 and a related species, the yellow azalea (*R. luteum*), in 1793. Much later arrivals include additional snowdrops (*Galanthus elwesii*) in 1874, glory-of-the-snow (*Chionodoxa siehei*) in 1877, additional crocuses (*Crocus ancyrensis*) in 1879, and reticulated irises (*Iris reticulata* var. *bakeriana, I. histrio* subsp. *aintabensis*) in 1887 and 1934.

Although some of these plants were native to Eastern Europe, it was not until the decline of the Ottoman Empire in the 19th century that Western botanists were easily able to access those regions to study their flora and fauna. The gardens of the West were transformed by the experiences of travelers to the Ottoman Empire who marveled at Ottoman gardens and the Turkish love of flowers and nature, and who brought these experiences—and plants—back with them to Western Europe.

A party in the harem garden from an 18th-century Ottoman album. A couple sitting side-by-side on stools are entertained by a group of musicians. Servants stand ready with a flask and fan. In the background are cypresses, flowering trees, and birds.

chapter III   Gardens in Ottoman Turkey

by Philippa Scott

When it fell to the Ottomans in spring of 1453, Constantinople had long been in disarray and poor repair, but it was always a city with public parks and private gardens. Its emperors and private citizens delighted in the orchards and flowering terraces they constructed and tended on its hills and along the Bosphorus shore. When Mehmed II captured the city, he set about rebuilding, reconstructing, and replanting the city that was to be the capital of a new, vibrant empire. Among its mosques today the visitor will find Laleli Camii (the Tulip Mosque) and Gül Camii (the Rose Mosque), originally an Orthodox church. Among the gardens and parks open to the public is Gülhane (the Park of the Rose), below the Topkapi Palace. Go today to Istanbul on a fine day in May, stroll through the great Spice Bazaar, and breathe the scent of freshly picked pink rose petals, heaped in baskets from dawn harvests. Early morning housewives buy these for their homemade rose-petal jam. Among the spice merchants and herbalists, find the specialists in attar of roses; lotions, creams, and beauty products manufactured from roses; and sacks of dried rosebuds for medicinal teas. The Byzantines made a liqueur from roses, and a rose *eau-de-vie* is made in Turkey today.

Ottoman architecture, wherever possible, incorporated gardens, and the traditional Ottoman garden, while linked to other gardens within the Islamic world, exhibits its own distinctive characteristics that emerged over the centuries. While each of these traditions developed its own garden style, water is central in all of them, for water is the source of life. What could Paradise be except a fertile garden nourished by the River of Life? Unlike the gardens in arid regions of Persia, India, and Spain, those of Istanbul were created where water existed and lie along the shore or on terraces sloping down to water. Sometimes gardens were made where no buildings existed, and where elaborate, beautifully colored and embroidered silk-hung tents, or pavilions, preceded kiosks, tent-like structures of stone and wood.

Kiosks, originally an Ottoman convention, became fashionable in the West in the Victorian Era. Garden founder Henry Shaw built a Turkish-inspired observatory in the Missouri Botanical Garden (above) and a Turkish pavilion in Tower Grove Park. (Photo courtesy MBG Archives.)

*The garden kiosk depicted is big enough for just one person and stands on
a platform of three steps. Its walls are clad with the hexagonal ceramic tiles.
Musicians provide entertainment beside a banquet.*

Kiosks (from the Turkish word *kosk*) were sometimes built to jut out over water, offering coolness in summer heat. Some kiosks were like roofed thrones, a seat with a view. Ottoman kiosks were much copied in the West, and many a bandstand in many a park, including those in London's Hyde Park, New York Central Park, and in St. Louis, Henry Shaw's Victorian gazebos in Tower Grove Park and the Garden, derive their design from these Turkish originals. In wooded areas in the sultans' hunting parks, a lodge sometimes became a palace at a later date. Ottoman paintings of palace gardens nearly always show Anatolian gazelles, birds, and rabbits among the trees and flowers. Gazelles and rabbits cropped the grass in open spaces used for sports such as archery and polo. Dovecotes supplied good garden fertilizer. Flowers, herbs, and vegetables were planted near each other to benefit from the proximity. For example, chickpeas or other legumes that emit nitrogen into the soil are beneficial to roses, and marigolds near carrots inhibit carrot fly.

There was a love of meandering paths in spaces that were very close to nature, with quiet recesses for sitting and appreciating nature and birdsong, as well as formal plantings in enclosed private gardens with geometric layouts. No garden was complete without cypresses and herbs among the flowers. Sometimes part of the Bosphorus shoreline was filled in to make a new, flat terrace for a waterside garden. Although today the royal hunting forests have given way to urbanization, there are still extensive municipal parks and woods, palace gardens, private gardens, and many garden shops and markets within present-day Istanbul, a city built along two shore lines, one in Europe and one in Asia.

To the Ottomans, any particularly beautiful garden was a Paradise Garden. An important source for historians of Ottoman garden history is the 17th-century traveler, Evliya Celebi, who described the places he visited, important buildings, characteristics of local building practices, gardens, trees and plants, and fountains. In these descriptions, most vegetation is described in general terms, but anything unusual or with medicinal properties is described in detail. He noted that plants from the New World were arriving and being grown in the Ottoman Empire, but unfortunately gives no specific details. It is almost impossible for us today to imagine Turkish food, or any other Mediterranean cuisine, before tomatoes were introduced from America. Tomatoes were first introduced to Turkey in the late 16th–17th century; however, they were eaten

In the Bakewell Ottoman Garden, a vibrant Rembrandt tulip stands out against a backdrop of euphorbia from which a bee takes nectar. Ottomans loved the sounds of the garden, including the "music" of bees. (Photo by Brent Johnston.)

green because it was thought that when they turned red they were spoiled. Tomatoes were categorized as a type of eggplant, and called *Firenk patlıcan*, i.e., Frankish, meaning foreign, eggplant. Other important American introductions include the potato, corn, tobacco, pepper, chili pepper, bell pepper, and pumpkin. Other ingredients we think of today as typically Mediterranean, such as the citrus family, apricots, peaches, and nectarines, arrived many centuries earlier from the Far East along the great trade routes we know collectively as the Silk Road. Myrtle was a favorite shrub in Byzantine and Ottoman gardens, appreciated for the fragrance of its modest flowers, and when black pepper, a precious and costly Asian luxury, was scarce, myrtle berries were substituted. The exchange in plant species encouraged trade, diplomatic endeavors and niceties, botanical studies, and scientific developments, and it was a feature of geographical and travel exploration.

Today, most people associate tulips with Holland, but the roots of this great Dutch success story were bulbs imported from the Ottoman Empire. A 16th-century Dutch traveler, Jehan Somer, wrote: "The Turks are great lovers of Gardens and herbs, and you would have to be a poor man not to have a little Garden. They spend much money on strange plants and flowers. Within Constantinople is a market where they sell nothing other than flowers and herbs, which are brought there from the Black Sea, or Mare Magiore, and from other places, from Egypt to India." From Constantinople he brought back "strange bulbs and herbs," many of which may be enjoyed in the Bakewell Ottoman Garden today. The Dutch turned the Ottoman appreciation of tulips into an obsession, and fortunes were made and lost. As still-life painting began to depict plants drawn from life, a school of Dutch flower paintings developed, and portraits of these gorgeous new flowers became a symbol of wealth. Although Rembrandt was a painter of portraits, not flowers, he lived and worked during the 17th-century "Tulipmania," and his name is now associated with those tulips with streaked and variegated petals. It was not until the 1930s that the random color breaking and mutation in some tulip petals was discovered to be caused by *potyvirus*, which causes a feathered and streaked appearance to the blooms. With identification of the cause and the aid of modern science, look-alike hybridized 'Rembrandt' tulips have been developed, with standardized color and petal combinations and types.

Among the wealth of trees, shrubs, and flowers long familiar in Western gardens introduced from the Ottoman Empire were many plants sought for practical as well as decorative purposes, such as medicines and dyes. The Ottomans were justly famous for their rugs, rich silks, and fine embroideries, and all dyes were obtained from natural sources. The famous "Turkey red" dye, *türk kırmızısı,* was obtained from the root of the madder plant. An intriguing document in British archives is a letter dated 1579, which urges that the English must learn how the Turks dyed wool, and in order to imitate this, an agent should send to England the plants used by the Turks "by seed or by root in barrels of earth."

Painted interior of the dome over the Sultan's throne in the Bakewell Ottoman Garden. The bold pattern and color are typical of the 19th-century Ottoman style. (Photo by Cara Smith.)

Each sultan made some addition to the seraglio gardens, either by laying out an entirely new garden or by the introduction of some previously unknown plants or trees. Ibrahim (r. 1640–1648) was particularly fond of tulips. His son, Mehmed IV (r. 1648–1687), loved all ranunculi, having roots and seeds sent by his pashas from all parts of Syria and the islands in the Mediterranean. Mustafa II (r. 1695–1703) was the first sultan to plant an imperial garden solely devoted to tulips, in the Fourth Court of the Topkapi Palace. He decreed that each new species of tulip should be registered and classified, and some beautiful tulip albums have survived, listing desirable qualities to be sought in tulips and the poetic names given to these flowers with almond-shaped bodies and tapering, elongated petals. Of all the flowers, the tulip was the best-loved, even appearing on Ottoman armor. Visitors to Istanbul remarked on the Turks' love of flowers, especially the tulip, and describe how they adorned their turbans with the flower.

Sultan Mustafa's son, Ahmed III, the "tulip king" (r. 1673–1736), inherited his father's passion for this flower. By the time of his reign, the city was buzzing with foreign embassies, and Dutch hybrid tulips appeared in Istanbul's markets and gardens. The sultan dispatched the first Ottoman ambassador to the French court, Yirmisekiz Mehmet Efendi, in 1720–21. Inspired by the plans and engravings of Fontainebleau and Versailles that his ambassador brought back from Paris, Sultan Ahmed III set about building five more palaces along the shores of the Bosphorus and the Golden Horn. The grandest and some say the most influenced by Versailles was Sa'adabad, or "Abode of Joy." A delightful example of Ottoman/French rococo is Sultan Ahmed III's Fountain (*Ahmet Çeşmesi*). Located in the great square in front of the Imperial Gate of Topkapi Palace, it was a popular place for people to meet and socialize in an informal setting. Above the drinking fountains and niches on each façade, stanzas of a poem dedicated to water are inscribed in fine calligraphy to be read clockwise around the fountain, and the inscription is bordered with decorative blue and red ceramic tiles. Although this is not one of his own poems, the sultan was a noted poet and calligrapher.

Violet and white Rembrandt-style "broken" tulips wave gracefully over a bed of silvery, fuzzy Stachys. Ottoman gardens are designed for total sensory experience: sight, smell, touch, sound, and taste. (Photo by Cindy Lancaster.)

Sultan Ahmed III had such a passion for tulips that his reign became known as the Tulip Era, and his extravagant fêtes were a drain on the national resources. In April, when the tulips were in bloom and the moon was full, lavish candlelit festivities were held to celebrate and enjoy the flowers. During the reign of Mahmud I, who succeeded Ahmed III, the tulip cult continued. A French observer has left a description of enclosed walkways through shelves of tulips, displayed singly, each in its own long-necked, bulbous-based vase, with cages of canaries and candlelight reflected through glass balls filled with colored liquids. He marveled at tortoises, which wandered among the visitors with candles fixed to their shells. The use of a tortoise-shaped base for royal monuments was common to both Turkish and Chinese mythology, symbolic of protection and longevity and evoking the Turks' origins in the east.

Palace gardens were tended by the Guild of Gardeners, at certain times numbering several thousand gardeners. The Head Gardener of the Topkapi Palace was a high ranking official, who doubled as head executioner. In case there were not enough heads to be chopped, another of his roles, doubtless more lucrative, was to supply wines to the foreign embassies.

Ottoman gardens frequently featured outdoor rooms within rooms, and silhouetted views were used to expand small spaces outward— and to offer new perspectives inward. (Photo by Kristen Peterson.)

Evergreens symbolized paradise to the Ottomans, and cypress colonnades were an essential part of Ottoman gardens. In the Bakewell Ottoman Garden, North American red cedar substitute for cypress, lining the allée in traditional style. (Photo by Kristen Peterson.)

chapter IV

Tour of the Bakewell Ottoman Garden

by Philippa Scott

As the visitor approaches the Bakewell Ottoman Garden, iron grille openings offer enticing views of the garden within. (For a plan of the garden, see pages 62–63.) The stately double-door gateway is set in an aged stucco wall and shaded by a gabled terra-cotta tile roof; a traditional Turkish tile panel mounted on the lintel proclaims in Arabic script, *"Al hamd li wali al hamd,"* "Praise to the Benefactor, Praise." Its companion panel, on the other side of the gateway, bids the visitor farewell, "The Benefactor awaits the reach of your memory within the garden." This, the last line of a contemporary Sufi poem by Kudsi Ergüner, has a double meaning, for the Benefactor refers to both the Creator of all, and Edward Bakewell, Jr. These verses set the mood of the space. Enter further, and the walled garden gently reveals its secrets, and hints at others. The mystical and shamanistic element, so attuned to nature, dominated the early Ottoman character and influenced their approach to gardens. Gardens were seen to reflect the pattern and order of the world, which was the work of the Creator.

In Ottoman court poetry, the garden was a metaphor for the inner world where the private, emotional part of human nature, hidden or suppressed in the daily, outer life, might be explored. Seeing a particularly beautiful tree or flower, the Ottoman also

The characteristic Ottoman red ochre doors to the Bakewell Ottoman Garden feature Turkish bronze accents that hint at the beauty within this walled garden. (Photo by Kristen Peterson.)

saw a faithful believer adoring God, and this beauty in nature reflected God's attention. To love nature and to appreciate God's creations was to offer prayers to God. They saw an important link between love and gardens; the scent of the rose signified the ineffable essence of the Divine, as in the poetry of the great 13th-century mystic, Celaleddin Rumi. In the Turkish city of Konya, a rose garden encloses the building that was his home and lodge, or *tekke*, and is now his mausoleum. The tiled surfaces of Ottoman mosques create gardens within gardens, ever-blooming flowers undulate on shimmering walls surrounded by the transitory flowers of this earthly realm. In Ottoman graveyards, which served as places for walking, sitting, and family picnics amid cypress trees and flowers, the gravestones of women were often denoted by flowers, usually roses or tulips, carved on the headstone.

Rumi founded the Mevlevi Order, the Whirling Dervishes, whose ecstatic dance is a prayer. The cure for those driven mad by earthly love, by yearnings and frustrations tied to more physical dimensions, was to be brought to a garden, sometimes forcibly, where they would be cured of this affliction by listening

to birds, music, and the soothing sounds of water, and by breathing deeply the scents of flowers and herbs.

Through the Bakewell Ottoman Garden gateway, the visitor is greeted by a mysterious Ottoman sundial, which stands just inside, with the reflecting pool beyond. Visitors pause here to take time and reflect on past, present, and future. (See pages 58–59 for a technical explanation of the many readings of an Ottoman sundial.)

Beyond the sundial, the immediate focal point is a shallow pool of water, or *havuz*, with a central fountain and small jets along its rim. Ottomans considered water to be the source of life. Proceeding to the right, a stone pedestal fountain, or *çeşme*, offers cool water within easy reach, and water gently drips along tiers of the wall fountain, *selsebil*. Both *çeşme* and *selsebil* have been specially made for the Garden from Turkish marble by traditional craftsmen in Turkey. Traditionally, music would play, the wistful sound of the Turkish flute, or *ney*, joining the tinkling rhythm of falling water. Many old Ottoman houses had special rooms with a central raised pool of water, which offered a cooling effect in the heat of summer, and sometimes a wall fountain near the entrance greeted those arriving and departing with its gentle music. It was considered an act of devotion to endow a public fountain, and a number of these were gifts from royal Ottoman women.

Continuing to the right, the visitor finds the plantings are well marked and clearly indicated. Wooden benches throughout the garden allow visitors to pause, linger, and take their ease and pleasure in the surroundings. Scent has been a priority in the selection of plants. Herbs are planted with flowers in the Ottoman manner, and perennials are placed in irregular groupings with overlaps to provide as natural an appearance as possible.

Previous Page: *As visitors enter the Bakewell Otoman Garden, they are invited to contemplate the heavens. A cerulean blue tile panel proclaims in Arabic calligraphy "Praise be to the Benefactor, Praise." (Photo by Kristen Peterson.)*

The çeşme, or pedestal fountain, offers visitors to the Bakewell Ottoman Garden cool water to wet their hands and brow. Water is a central feature in Ottoman gardens, symbolizing the rivers of paradise. (Photo by Erin Whitson.)

The formal beds flanking the pool have plantings that change seasonally, offering colorful hyacinths (*Hyacinthus orientalis*), tazetta narcissi (*Narcissus* spp.), and carnations (*Dianthus caryophyllus*) in spring, to be replaced by a shimmer of summer- and fall-flowering pot marigolds (*Calendula officinalis*) in yellow, gold, and orange. Ottoman hyacinths, depicted on so many Iznik tile panels and embroideries, were originally delicate flowers, only blue or white, quite different from the profusely blossomed, multihued varieties with which we are familiar today. Their perfume, however, is unchanged. In winter, tender plants will be taken inside one of the Garden's greenhouses, just as in Ottoman palace gardens orange and lemon trees in large pots and urns were protected from winter frost inside the greenhouse, or *limonluk*. The Ottoman Garden's large pots contain pomegranate (*Punica granatum* 'Wonderful'), jasmine (*Jasminum sambac*), and

*Yarrow (*Achillea *'Coronation Gold') gives a splash of vivid yellow, one of many massed plantings in the Bakewell Ottoman Garden done for colorful effect in the traditional Ottoman style. (Photo by Leslie Wallace.)*

Pomegranate trees are grown in pots in the Bakewell Ottoman Garden. They feature beautiful red flowers in spring and an equally attractive fruit later in the year, filled with ruby-colored seeds. (Photo by Cara Smith.)

Meyer lemon (*Citrus × meyeri* 'Meyer'). Pomegranate has a bright red flower in spring, and as a symbol of fertility and fruitfulness was a popular motif on embroideries. Left unpicked on the tree, the fruit eventually burst open with a cracking noise, sending the seeds forth to do as nature intends.

The Bakewell Ottoman Garden presents plants native to the terrain and territories of the expansive Ottoman Empire whenever possible, but also includes a few non-native plants that would have been grown in the 16th through 19th centuries in what is now Turkey. The Asian persimmon (*Diospyros kaki*) from China and the red-flowered mimosa tree (*Albizia julibrissin*), which ranged from Iran to China and Korea, were highly regarded ornamental exotics during the Ottoman period.

By the brochure box, columbine (*Aquilegia vulgaris*) grows next to magenta-hued rose campion (*Lychnis coronaria*). Clumps of colorful primroses (*Primula* spp.) and a beautiful blue monkshood known as Arend's Turk's cap (*Aconitum carmichaelii* 'Arendsii') fill out the corner where the North American native persimmon (*Diospyros virginiana*), common throughout Missouri, has been planted in lieu of the non-hardy Caucasian persimmon, also known as the date-plum (*Diospyros lotus*). During the summer months, visitors should pause to enjoy the exquisite fragrance of the colorful oleander trees (*Nerium oleander*) grouped in front of the windows. The next bed, edged with boxwood (*Buxus sempervirens*), includes a wild pear (*Pyrus communis* 'Moonglow'), foxgloves (*Digitalis grandiflora*), Portland rose (*Rosa* 'Jacques Cartier'), prickly comfrey (*Symphytum asperum*), and several apple trees chosen for their shape and modest growth: *Malus pumila* 'Obelisk,' 'Trajan,' and 'Tuscan.' Golden yarrow (*Achillea* 'Coronation Gold') gives a splash of vivid yellow.

From the far right corner along the north wall, approaching the grape arbor and its vines, is a stand of Turkish spuria iris (*Iris orientalis*), continuing across in plots on either side of the arbor's front steps with plantings of milky bellflower (*Campanula lactiflora*), clumps of spurge (*Euphorbia myrsinites*), Caucasus poppy (*Papaver oreophyllum*), bold-leaved acanthus (*Acanthus spinosus*), and many varieties of species geranium (*Geranium* spp.). Another pear tree (*Pyrus communis*) and Damask rose (*Rosa* 'Rose de Rescht') stand directly opposite the Portland rose and wild pear and, over time, additional old roses will be planted.

Two birdhouses, or *kuşevi*, on the north wall invite occupancy, however fleeting, of a feathered nature. The wooden grape arbor, or *çardak*, covers a raised paved patio against the back wall of the garden. Its beamed trellis with painted wooden column caps is dominated by a copper dome topped with a brass tulip-shaped finial, or *alem*. The dome's interior is painted with

delicate tracery. The murals along the back wall of the grape arbor are copied from Ottoman depictions in manuscripts. Pavilions and interiors frequently had painted wooden roofs and wall panels showing flowers, murals with country scenes, scenes with ships, terraced gardens with kiosks, or indoor images which reflect what might be seen gazing out from the windows. Ottoman paintings frequently show wooden lattices and doors painted with red ochre, a custom the Turks brought with them from Central Asia and beyond. Describing the marvelous court of Tamerlane in Samarkand, the 15th-century Spanish ambassador Ruy de Clavijo remarked on the cinnabar paling used as a garden fence.

A carved Ottoman-style baluster marks the outer edge of the grape arbor so the visitor might lean there or take their ease on the carved seat and, from the arbor's raised perspective, gaze down onto the reflecting pool, or across to the entrance, to view and enjoy the entire garden from a different perspective. Some plantings will change according to the season; others will change as the garden evolves and matures.

The carved seat on the patio takes its design from traditional Ottoman thrones. Wooden ones like this were transportable. An interesting marble example, similarly shaped, stands behind the Head Physician's Tower in the terrace gardens of the Topkapi Palace's Fourth Court. Originally a 6th-century Byzantine bishop's throne, the sultan would sit here to watch sporting events taking place in the garden. Looking down on that palace terrace are two lovely wooden pavilions, from which honored guests, family members, or the sultan's harem could discreetly watch and admire archery, javelin throwing, feats of horsemanship, and similar activities.

The rear double doors are used as the garden entrance for special events, and from this point the pathway leads gently back toward the main entrance through the "cypress allée." A typical Ottoman cypress walkway is represented here by a columnar selection of the North American red cedar (*Juniperus virginiana* 'Taylor'), which offers a similar visual presentation. (Mediterranean cypress does not flourish in the St. Louis

Ottoman gardens were places for contemplation of both flora and fauna. The Bakewell Ottoman Garden has two traditional birdhouses (kuşevi) to invite songbirds to take up occupancy. (Photo by Kristen Peterson.)

climate.) Cypress is grown in graveyards in the old Ottoman dominions as a reminder of mortality, and it was often planted to commemorate a death, though it was also much loved because of it elegant, sculptural form. The cypress finds its way into Ottoman designs almost as often as the tulip. Traditionally, rosemary (*Rosmarinus officinalis*) was planted around the base of cypresses, especially if these lined an avenue, offering a unified expanse of green. In the Bakewell Ottoman Garden, rosemary and furry, silvery lamb's ear (*Stachys byzantina*) grow with the red cedars, which face a yew hedge along the opposite wall. Another fruit tree, the sweet cherry (*Prunus avium* 'Stanley'), has been planted, and more large pots stand here. The informal beds include oregano (*Origanum vulgare*), which mingles with knapweed (*Centaurea dealbata*), betony (*Stachys* spp.), lavender (*Lavandula angustifolia*), irises (*Iris* spp.), oriental poppies (*Papaver orientale*), hollyhocks (*Alcea* spp.), and yellow pincushion flowers (*Cephalaria gigantea*). The formal beds beside the pool, lined with miniature germander hedges (*Teucrium chamaedrys*), have seasonal bulbs and annuals which change throughout the year.

Visitors should keep an eye out for a few special plants which are not commercially available and were collected by Garden horticulture staff during an expedition to Turkey's neighboring Republic of Georgia. These include *Cephalaria gigantea*, *Papaver oreophilum*, and *Symphytum asperum*, among others. Finally, at the end of the walkway fringed with dark-leaved yew and cedar, the visitor arrives back at the sundial and the entrance gateway.

Different cultures have seen gardens in very different ways, but a garden is always a place to experience new and familiar delights, and to remember those past. Like all of life, gardens are constantly changing and evolving. Plants grow, come to fruition, die, and are reborn from their seeds. The Bakewell Ottoman Garden offers a place of renewal where visitors may experience contemplation, reverie, tranquility, and refuge. The scents, shapes, colors, and shades of plants delight the senses, lift the spirits, ease the heart, and evoke the reach of your memory.

*Traditional hollyhocks (*Alcea *spp.) in the Bakewell Ottoman Garden mirror the upward thrust of the fountain jets of the* havuz, *or central fountain. In Ottoman symbolism, they lead visitors' thoughts upward to paradise and the "Heavenly Gardener." (Photo by Leslie Wallace.)*

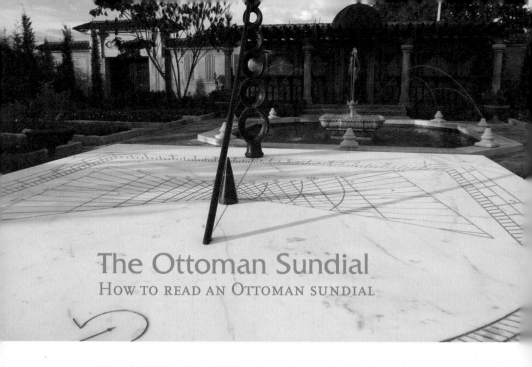

The Ottoman Sundial
HOW TO READ AN OTTOMAN SUNDIAL

The sundial has four different sets of time lines. The secret to reading is to start with 12 o'clock in each system:

> At 12 western time (noon), the shadow points due north.
> At 12 Babylonian, the shadow is due east.
> At 12 Italian, it is due west.

On the outer dial showing western hours, 12 o'clock is noon and the shadow from the slanted rod (polar gnomon) is exactly under the gnomon and points north along the north-south axis.

WESTERN EUROPEAN TIME
In the western European time system, the starting point for the day is midnight and noon in 12 hour cycles, a.m. and p.m. Count afternoon hours clockwise toward the east. Count down counter clockwise from 12 for the morning hours on the west. The same applies for Babylonian and Italian hours, but the 12 o'clock lines are on an east-west line parallel to the equinox declination line and south of the base of the vertical gnomon.

ITALIAN TIME
The day starts and ends at sunset for Italian time. This 12 o'clock (zero) cannot be shown on a horizontal dial as the shadow is infinitely long at sunset. The last Italian hour shown on the east side of the dial is 11 o'clock in the evening, one hour before

sunset. Count down from 11 going counter clockwise until the line is due west at zero or 12 o'clock in the morning. In the longer days of summer the count continues down from 12 until sunrise.

BABYLONIAN TIME

The system is exactly the same for Babylonian hours, but in reverse as their day starts and ends at sunrise. The first Babylonian hour shown is one hour after sunrise, 1 o'clock on the far west of the dial. The Babylonian hours count clockwise and the lines slant over more to the east until 12 o'clock in the afternoon when the sun is due west and the shadow due east. Again, in the summer when the number of daylight hours is more than 12, the count begins again so the next line sloping south of east is 1 o'clock again. (Note: Babylonian hours are not engraved on the dial as they would be confusing compared with conventional hours.)

In the western system noon is fixed and sunrise and sunset times vary with the seasons. In Babylonian hours, sunrise is fixed and the time of mid-day (noon) and sunset varies. In Italian hours sunset is fixed and the time of mid-day (noon) and sunrise vary with the seasons.

On the spring and fall equinox, when the day is 12 hours from sunrise to sunset, all the systems show the same time on a true Ottoman sundial where noon is 6 o'clock. On this dial, 12 is shifted to noon in line with western time conventions.

Muslim prayer times are determined by the length of the shadow compared to the length at noon when the shadow is shortest, and the muezzin calls the faithful to prayer from the top of the mosque's minaret. The noon prayer (*zuhr*) starts as soon as the shadow begins to lengthen. This is taken as the noon length plus one-fourth the height of the gnomon. The afternoon prayer (*asr*) starts when the shadow length is the noon height plus the height of the gnomon and ends when the shadow is the noon height plus twice the gnomon height.

The Ottoman sundial in the Bakewell Ottoman Garden. It serves an important function as an indicator of Muslim prayer requirements, but also invites visitors to consider the passage of time. (Photo by Jamison Ford.)

Plants of the Bakewell Ottoman Garden

Plant names are presented in Latin followed by their English common name in parentheses and their common name in modern Turkish. Plants vary seasonally over time. Not all plants are on display year-round.

HERBACEOUS MATERIAL FOR LATE SPRING-LATE FALL INTEREST

Acanthus spinosus (bear's breeches) – Dikenli ayı pençesi
Achillea spp. (yarrow) – civan perçemi
Aconitum spp. (Monk's hood) – kurtboğanotu
Alcea pallida and *A. rugosa* (hollyhock) – hatmi çiçeği
Aquilegia vulgaris (columbine) – haseki küpesi
Asphodeline lutea, A. liburnica (king's spear) – sarı çirişotu
Calendula officinalis (pot marigold) – portakal nergisi, Karagöz, aynisafa
Campanula spp. (milky bellflower) – çan çiçeği
Centaurea dealbata (bachelor's button) – peygamber çiçeği
Cephalaria gigantea (giant pincushion flower) – Gösterisli pelemir
Dianthus spp. (carnation) – karanfil
Digitalis spp. (foxglove) – yüksük otu
Euphorbia myrsinites (spurge) – sütleğen
Geranium sanguineum, 'Album' (hardy geranium) – Turna gagası
Hyssopus officionalis, H. aristatus (hyssop) – zulfa otu
Lathyrus latifolius (sweet pea) – bezelye
Lavandula angustifolium (lavender) – lavanta
Lavatera trimestris (rose mallow) – pembe ebegümeci
Leucanthemum × *superbum* (Shasta daisy) – margarit papatya
Lychnis coronaria (catchfly) – yalancı karanfil, ibrik çiçeği
Nigella damascene (love-in-a-mist) – çörek otu
Origanum vulgare (oregano) – mercanköşk
Papaver oreopyllum, P.orientale hybrids (poppy) – Türk gelinciği
Primula spp. (primrose) – çuha çiçeği
Rosmarinus officinalis (rosemary) – biberiye
Stachys byzantina, S. officinalis (lamb's ear) – tibbi kestere
Symphytum asperum (borage) – hodan, kabakafes otu
Teucrium chamaedrys (germander) – kısa mahmut otu, yer meşesi

GEOPHYTIC MATERIAL FOR SPRING-FALL INTEREST

Colchicum spp. (colchicum) – güz çiğdemi
Crocus spp. (crocus) – safran
Cyclamen spp. (cyclamen) – siklamen
Galanthus spp. (snowdrop) – kardelen

As visitors exit the Bakewell Ottoman Garden, the inscription invokes the divine, as well as wittily thanking the donor and caretakers of the garden. Written in Ottoman script in gold on the blue tile: "The Benefactor awaits the reach of your memory within the garden." (Photo by Jack Jennings.)

Hyacinthus orientalis blue, white, and pink selections
   (hyacinth) – Türk sümbülü
Iris spp. (iris) – mor süsen
Lilium candidum (lily) – beyaz zambak
Muscari spp. (grape hyacinth) – Dağ sümbülü
Narcissus tazetta hybrids (narcissus) – nergiz
Paeonia spp. (peony) – şakayık, Avigülü
Scilla spp. (squill) – ada soğanı
Sternbergia spp. (autumn daffodil) – sarı ciğdem
Tulipa spp. and assorted historic hybrids (tulip) – lale

WOODY MATERIAL FOR YEAR-ROUND INTEREST

Albizia julibrissin (mimosa) – gülibrişim
Buxus sempervirens (boxwood) – Anadolu Şimşiri
Citrus spp. (lemon) – limon
Cornus mas (cornelian cherry) – kızılcık
Ficus carica (fig) – incir ağacı
Hibiscus styracifolia (rose of Sharon) – ağac hatmi
Jasminum sambac (jasmine) – yasemin
Juniperus virginiana 'Taylor' (cedar) – sedir
Malus spp. (apple) – elma ağacı
Nerium oleander selections (oleander) – zakkum
Prunus spp. (plum) – erik ağacı
Punica granata 'Wonderful' (pomegranate) – nar
Pyrus spp. (pear) – armut ağacı
Rosa selections of Portland and Damask hybrids (rose) – gül
Vitis spp. (grape) – üzüm, asma

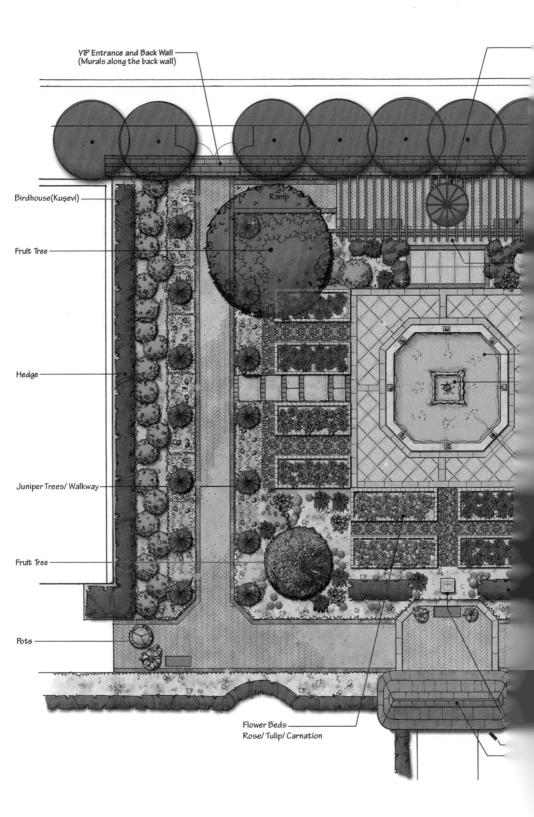

VIP Entrance and Back Wall
(Murals along the back wall)

Birdhouse(Kuşevi)

Fruit Tree

Ramp

Hedge

Juniper Trees/ Walkway

Fruit Tree

Pots

Flower Beds
Rose/ Tulip/ Carnation

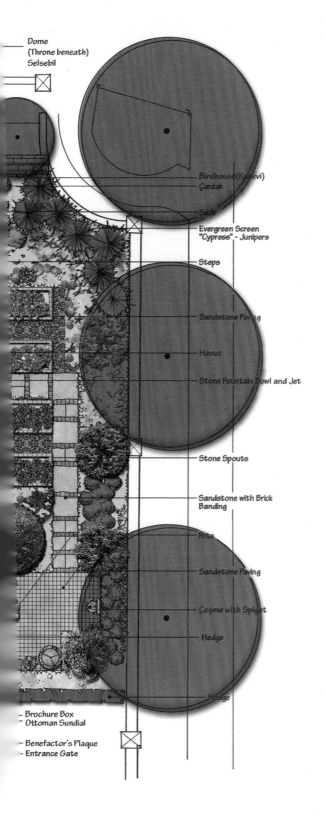

Dome
(Throne beneath)
Selsebil

Birdhouse(Kuşevi)
Çardak

Sed

Evergreen Screen
"Cypress" - Junipers

Steps

Sandstone Paving

Havuz

Stone Fountain Bowl and Jet

Stone Spouts

Sandstone with Brick
Banding

Pots

Sandstone Paving

Çeşme with Spigot

Hedge

Hedge

Brochure Box
Ottoman Sundial

Benefactor's Plaque
Entrance Gate

BAKEWELL OTTOMAN GARDEN

BENEFACTOR
Edward L. Bakewell, Jr.

CONCEPT & COORDINATION
Anderson D. Bakewell
Edward L. Bakewell III

ARCHITECTURE & DESIGN
Fazil Sutcu, AIA

ARCHITECTURAL,
HORTICULTURAL, &
HISTORICAL CONCEPT
Prof. Nikos Stavroulakis

SPECIAL CONSULTING
Prof. Nurhan Atasoy

GENERAL CONTRACTING
BSI Constructors, Inc.

ARTIFACT SOURCING
Burhan Karabulut

DECORATIVE PAINTING
Fishing Creek Studios
Semih Irteş
Grace E. McCammond

SUNDIAL
Abraham Mohler

CALLIGRAPHY
Hasan Çelebi

HISTORICAL CONSULTING
Prof. Gülru Necipoğlu

HORTICULTURAL REALIZATION
Jason Delaney

INITIAL PROJECT
COORDINATION
MTR Landscape Architects

Dedication

EDWARD L. BAKEWELL, JR.

1916–1993

*"The Benefactor awaits
the reach of your memory
within the garden."*